The 5th LAST Festival

Presented by Stanford University at the SLAC National Accelerator Laboratory

"Almost anything that we create can become monstrous. One hopes for the best, but never knows just how it might play out. The story of humankind is partially a history of the twists and turns posited by technological innovation. The complex relationship between intention and context sometimes converge in mysterious and unpredictable ways resulting in new creative strategies, machines, social architectures, designs and creative expression."
-*Joel Slayton*

About LAST Festival

The LAST (Life Art Science Technology) festival celebrates the confluence of art with the new media technologies and nascent sciences that are transforming sociality and experience in the 21st century.

Creativity does not happen in a vacuum, whether it's art, tech or science. They all coexist, influence each other and interact. Silicon Valley did not happen in a vacuum, it happened within the intense cultural ecosystem of the Bay Area. The LAST festival aims at presenting art, tech and science within the same venue. The art exhibition features interactive high-tech installations that break the "Do not touch!" taboo of the traditional museum and that are meant to let you experience something you never experienced before. The speakers features talks on Artificial Intelligence, Graphics/Animation, Nanotech, Space Exploration, Computer Graphics, etc by leaders of today's science and technology.

-Piero Scaruffi, LAST Festival Founder

About SLAC

As one of 17 Department of Energy national labs, SLAC National Accelerator Laboratory pushes the frontiers of human knowledge and drives discoveries that benefit humankind. SLAC invents the tools that make those discoveries possible and shares them with scientists all over the world. Four Nobel prizes have been awarded for work at SLAC, which is operated by Stanford University for the DOE.

Artists

Jonathon Keats
Kal Spelletich
Scott Kildall
Carlos Castellanos
Purin Phanichph
Amy Karle
Gary Boodhoo
Raul Altosaar

Melanie Piech
Raphael Arar
Mobile Arts Platform
Cesar & Lois
Pantea Karimi
Tony Assi
Brian Reinbolt
Daniel Stefanescu

Anja Ulfeldt
Kathleen Deck
Jiaqi Zhag & Anton va Beek
Alex Reben
Steve Durie

Festival Speakers

Michael Snyder
Melissa Merencillo
Steve Omonhundro
Alison Gopnik
Ken Goldberg
Maya Ackerman
Piero Scaruffi
Vivenne Ming

Performances

Andrew Blanton
Rob Hamilton &
Chris Platz

Hand Shaker

Kal Spelletich

Robotic hand senses a human and extends an open hand. Upon contact, it decides according to your heartbeat and touch which of three grip strengths to use. It decides when and how often to shake hands and when to let go.

Kal's work explores the boundaries between fear, control, and exhilaration. For 25 years, he has been experimenting with interfacing humans and robots with humans using technology to put people back in touch with intense real life experiences and to empower them. Kal's work is always interactive, requiring a participant to enter or operate the piece, often against their instincts of self-preservation

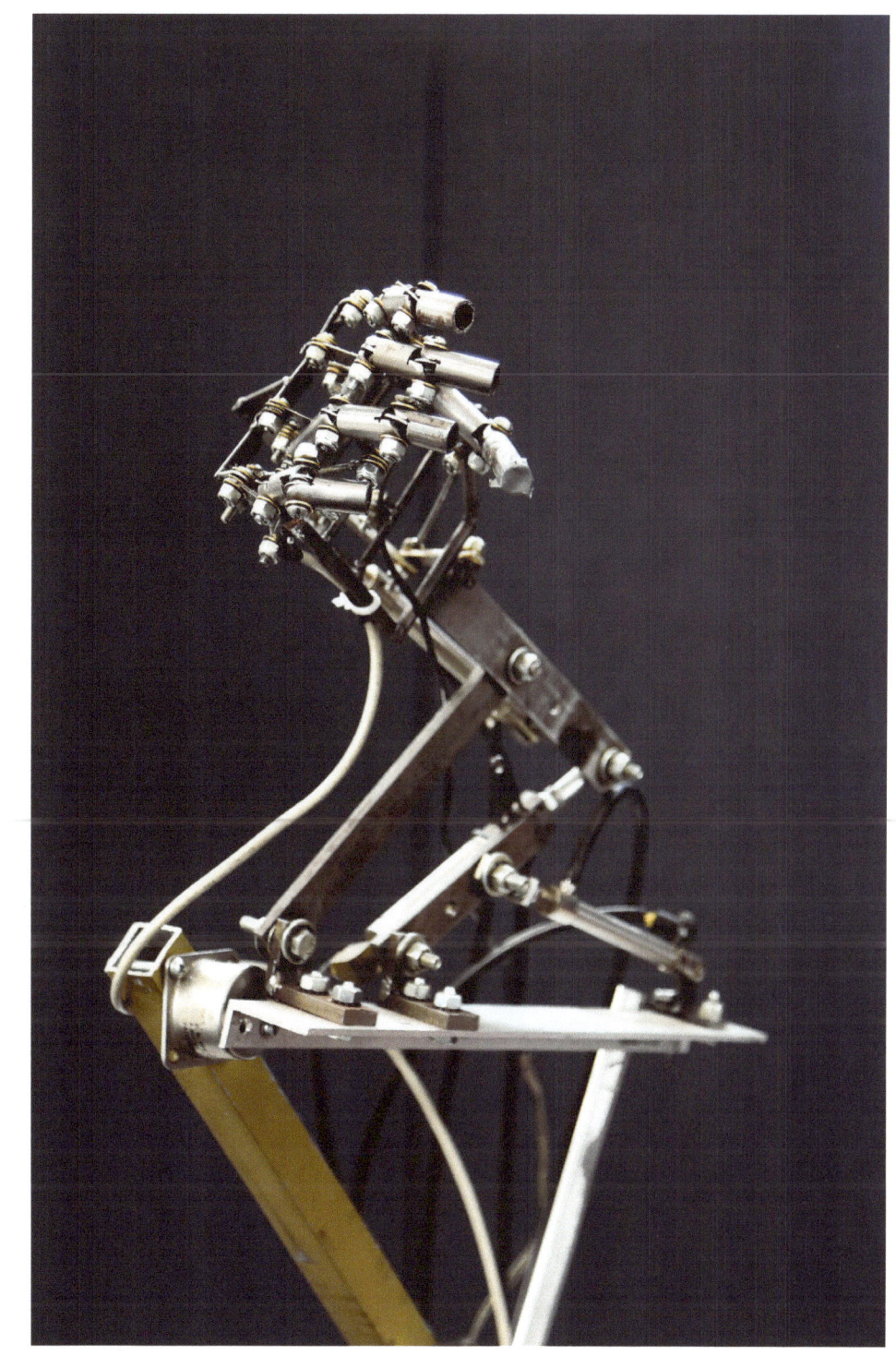

NASA, NorCal Artists Seeking America

The Mobile Arts Platform (MAP)

Artists Peter Foucault and Chris Treggiari are Factronauts, part of a special exploration program called NASA, NorCal Artists Seeking America. Their mission, to seek out information and stories that will help illuminate this post-election county that has been turned on its ear. This project is a collaboration with filmmakers Bryan and Vita Hewitt.

The Mobile Arts Platform (MAP) is a Bay Area artmaking and curatorial team founded in 2009 by Peter Foucualt and Chris Treggiari with the goal of creating mobile exhibition structures that engage the public. MAP creates an autonomous exhibition space, an artistic research lab where a cross pollination of mediums and genres can occur, be accessible to the public, and create strong bonds with partner communities.

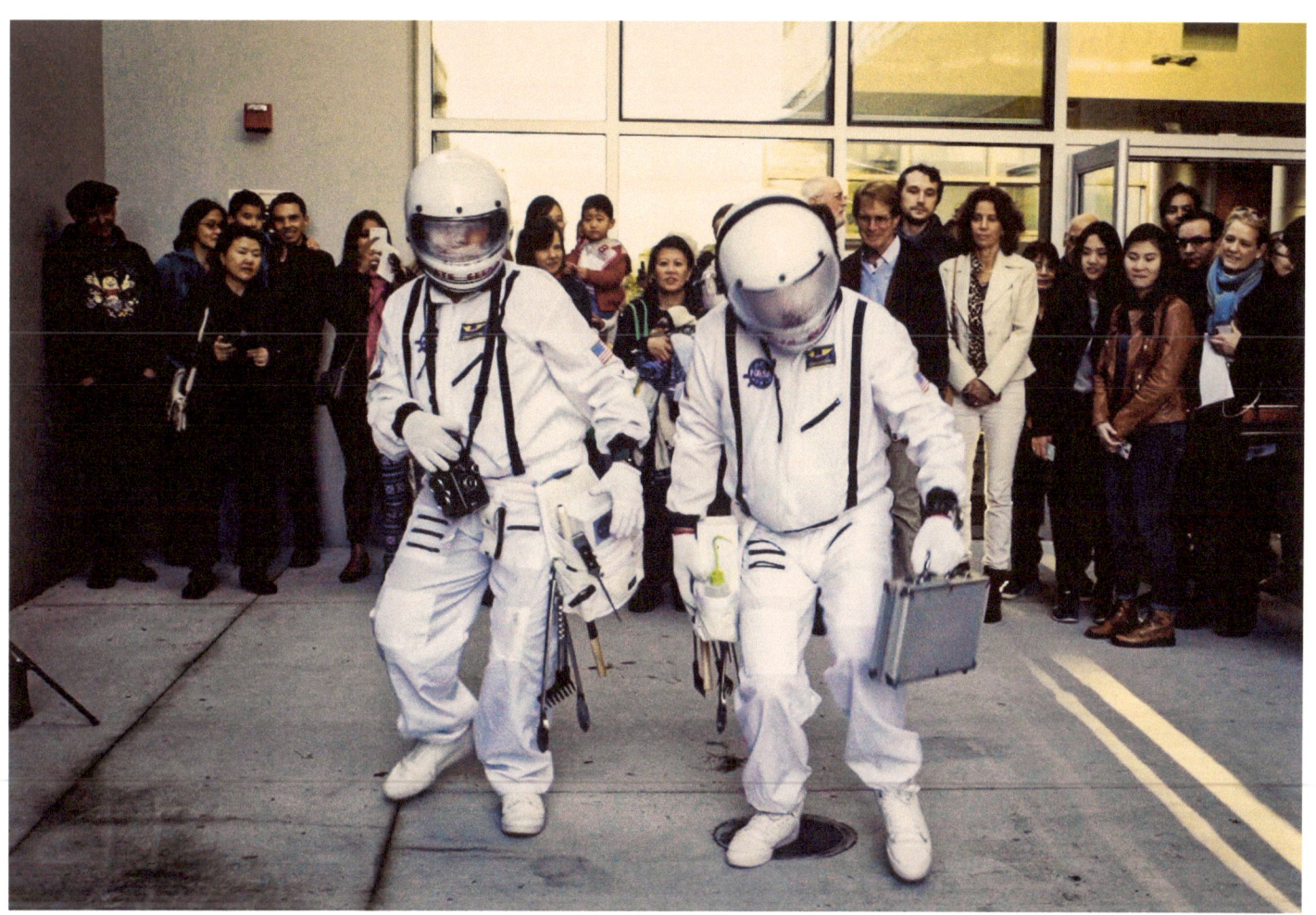

Free Will (Placebo)

Jonathon Keats

Morality depends on free will. However research in fields ranging from neuroscience to physics shows that human behavior and the universe as a whole may be deterministic. In the interest of protecting human morals, and promoting civic responsibility in democratic society, experimental philosopher Jonathon Keats has made an important breakthrough in pharmacology: a placebo for free will that may be taken orally. The only known antidote for determinism, this ethical placebo will be made freely available through a free will dispensary at the LAST Festival.

Jonathon Keats is an experimental philosopher, writer, and artist. His conceptually-driven interdisciplinary art projects, hosted by institutions ranging from Arizona State University to the Los Angeles County Museum of Art, include the creation of a photosynthetic restaurant for plants and the development of cameras that take thousand-year-long exposures, documenting the long-term effects of climate change. Keats is the author of six books, most recently You Belong to the Universe: Buckminster Fuller and the Future, published by Oxford University Press. He is a Research Fellow at the Nevada Art Museum's Center for Art + Environment, and the Black Mountain College Legacy Fellow at the University of North Carolina - Asheville.

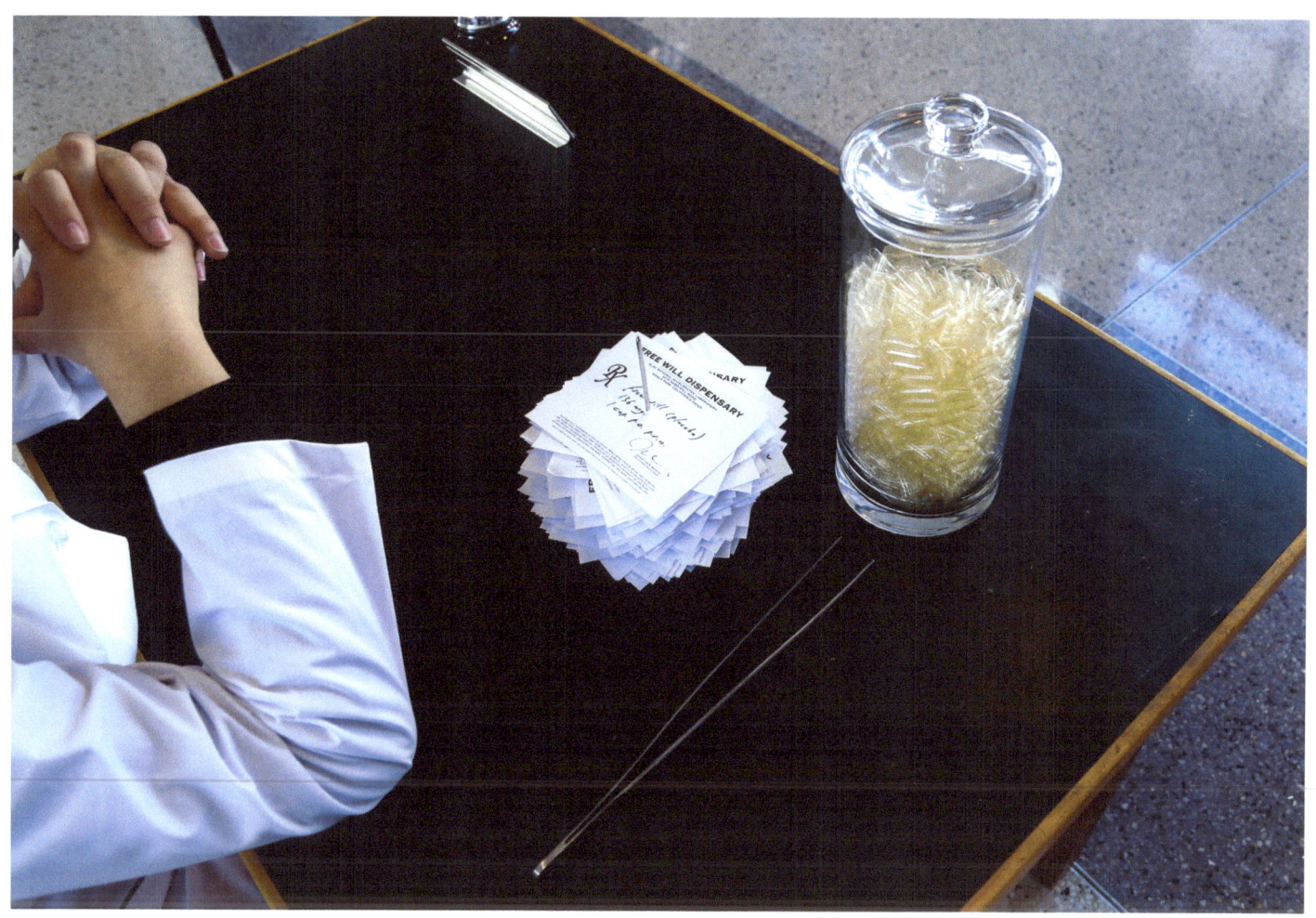

Populace Guise

Alexander Reben

Over 5 million faces used to train facial recognition systems without consent.

Alexander Reben is an artist and roboticist, who explores humanity through the lens of art and technology. His work deals with human-machine relationships, synthetic psychology, artificial philosophy, and robot ethics, among other topics. Using "art as experiment," his work allows for the viewer to experience the future within metaphorical contexts. Rueben's artwork and research have been shown and published internationally, and he consults with major copanies, guiding innovation for the social machine future.

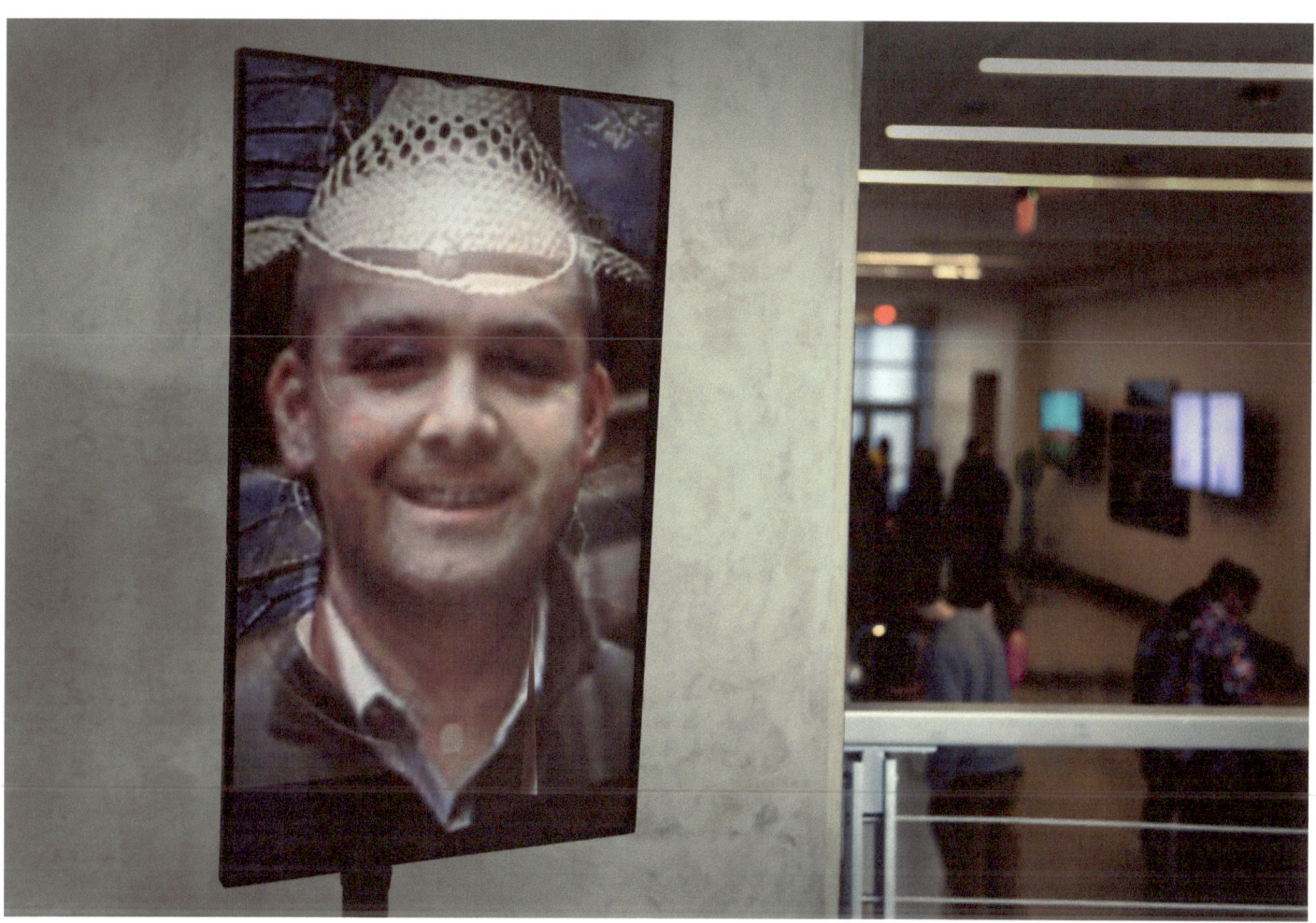

Cybernetic Spirits

Scott Kildall

Cybernetic Spirits is an interactive electronic artwork where participants can generate sonic arrangements by "playing" fluids that humans worship in our contemporary society such as coffee, adrenaline, breast milk, blood and gasoline.

Scott Kildall is cross-disciplinary artist who writes algorithms that transform various datasets into 3D sculptures and installations. The resulting artworks often invite public participation through direct interaction.

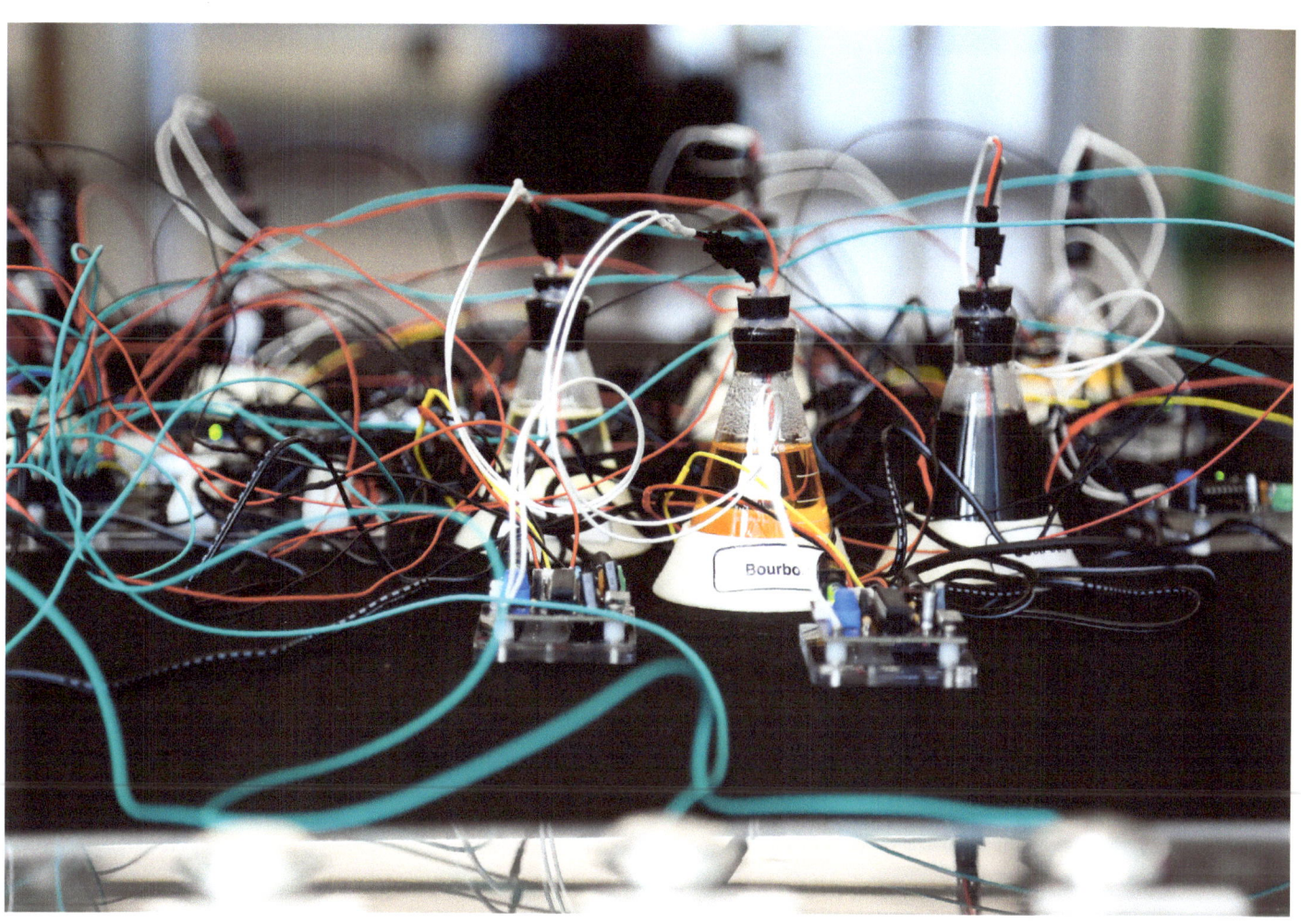

Nostalgia

Raphael Arar

Nostalgia is an installation that draws attention to the computational challenges of understanding human emotion, specifically the sentiment it refers to. By sharing a memory, the installation will rank the nostalgic strength of your entry based on its underlying AI-driven nostalgia index. Its interpretation will be communicated back in physical and digital forms.

Raphael Arar is an award-winning artist, designer and technologist whose work elucidates the complexities of human-machine relationships. His artwork has been shown at museums, conferences, festivals, and galleries internationally including the International Symposium on Electronic Art (ISEA), ACM CHI Conference on Human Factors in Computing Systems, Gamble House Museum, Boston Cyberarts Gallery, and the Athens Video Art Festival.

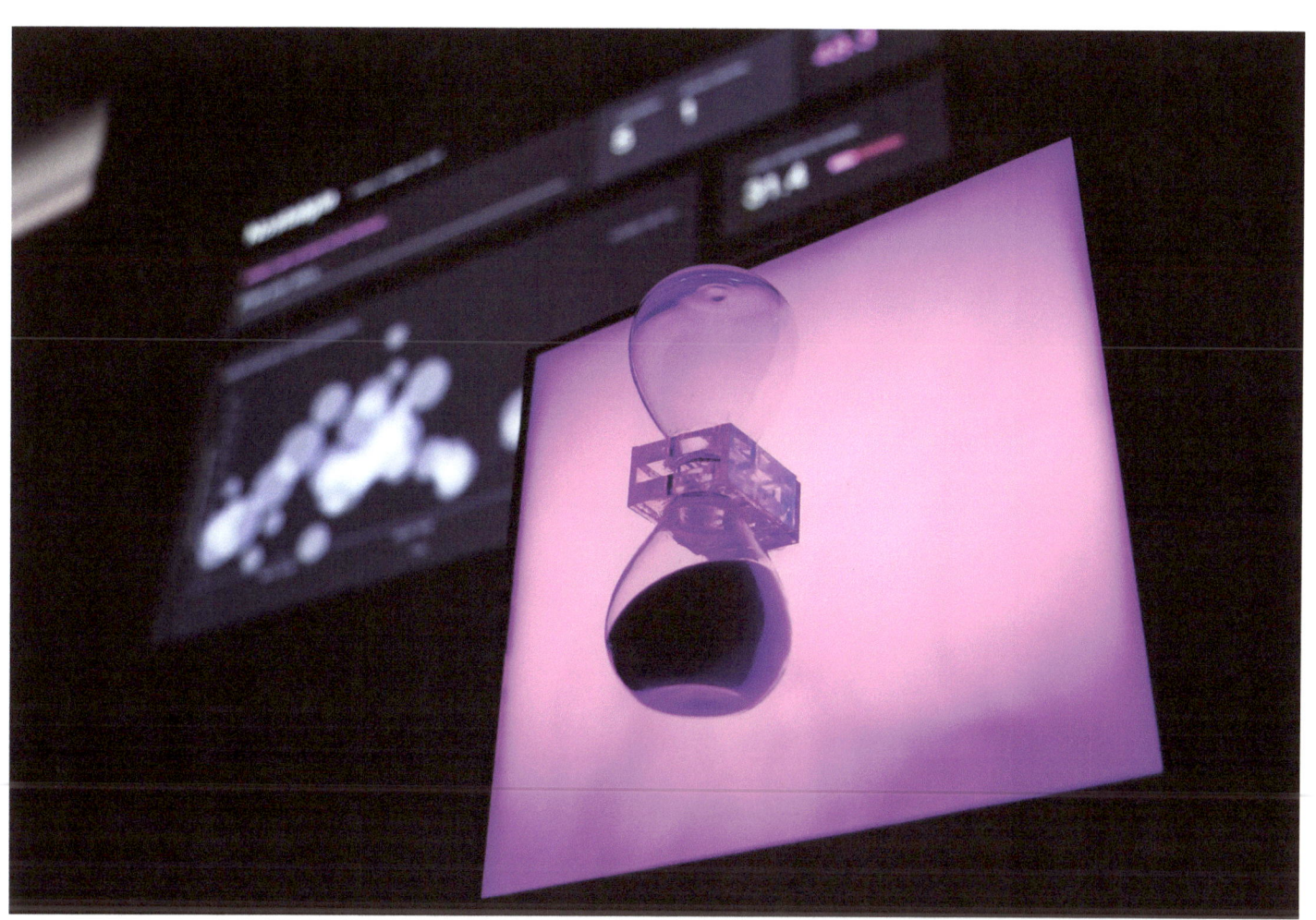

Progress Accelerated

Daniel Stefanescu

Is an attempt to direct the viewer's sentiment to man's seemingly inevitable arrival at a synthetic future of his own making. Four animated composites are viewed as holographic tableaus, each confined within a pyramidal vignette. The imagery is heavily symbolic and reminiscent of a time period in human development and passively infers its meaning by associating readily identifiable imagery.

Daniel Stefanescu manages the technical and logistical requirements of the XPP hard X-ray instrument at the SLAC National Accelerator Laboratory. His background is in cryogenics and ultra-high vacuum science. He is also a graduate of the San Jose State University School of Business and holds a minor in Graphic Design.

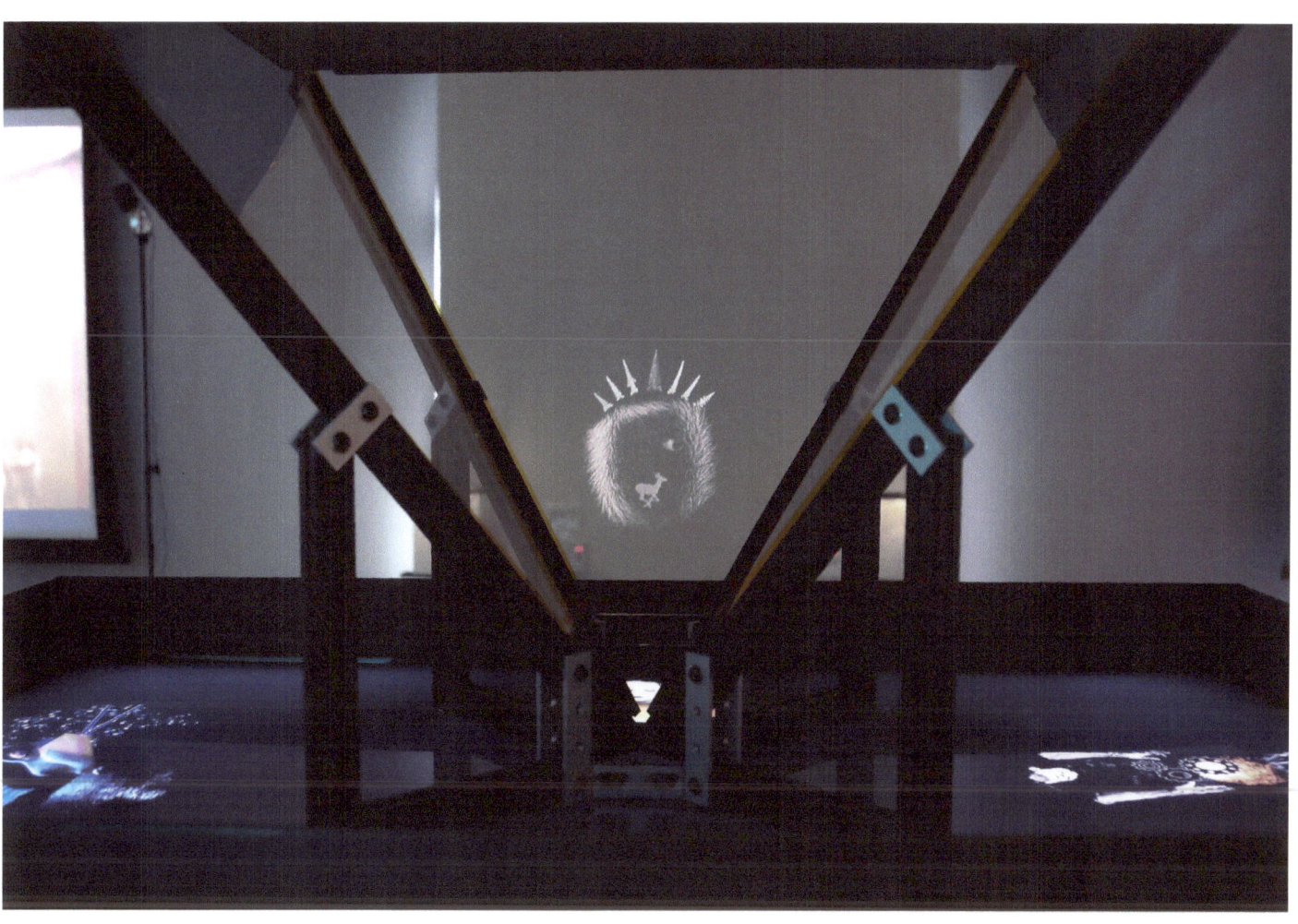

Gaze Relations

Tony Assi

Gaze Relations illustrates the difference between how people and computer vision algorithms perceive the body. Gaze tracking demonstrates the complexity of human perception in comparison with body detection algorithms that reduce the body to simple patterns, revealing and contrasting the processes of human and machine vision.

Tony Assi is a Digital Arts + New Media MFA student at the University of California, Santa Cruz working at the intersection of visual art and computer vision. Tony uses visual art and software to investigate the relationship between people and technology through critical visualizations.

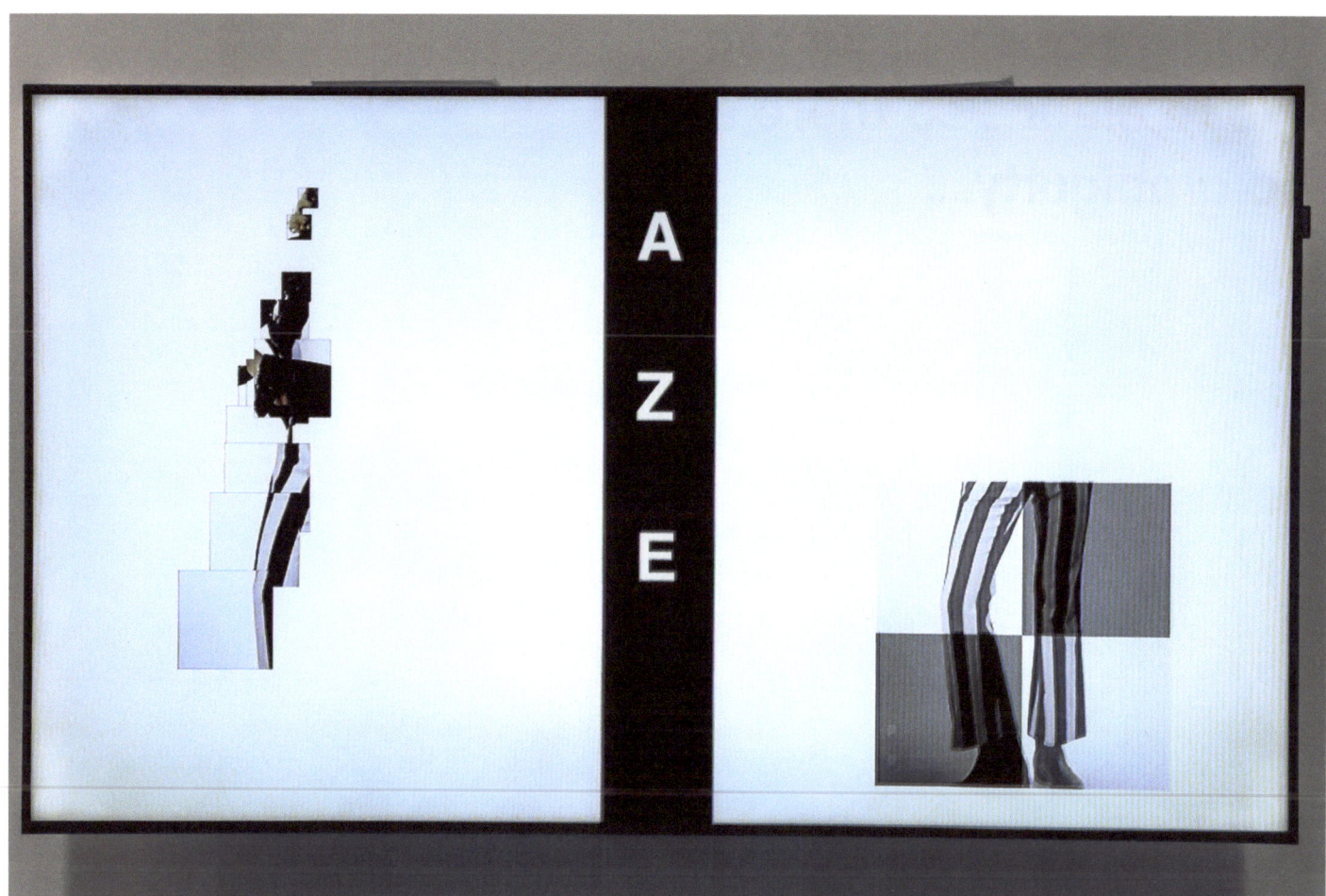

"No," means no... just so we're clear... so there's no ambiguity....

Melanie Piech

What if, starting from the very beginning of time, women were not thought of (by some) as prey? How would the power imbalance be changed? This piece represents these ideas...a prototype for a piece of wearable tech for women. Its blades triggered in response to a stress sensor.

Melanie Piech uses sculpture to explore questions about our individual human and collective societal experience. She returns to themes of time's passage, female-ness including gender-equality, and social justice. She aims to encourage people to ruminate about their lives and how we fit together in our society, to engage others in discussion, even if it is only in their heads.

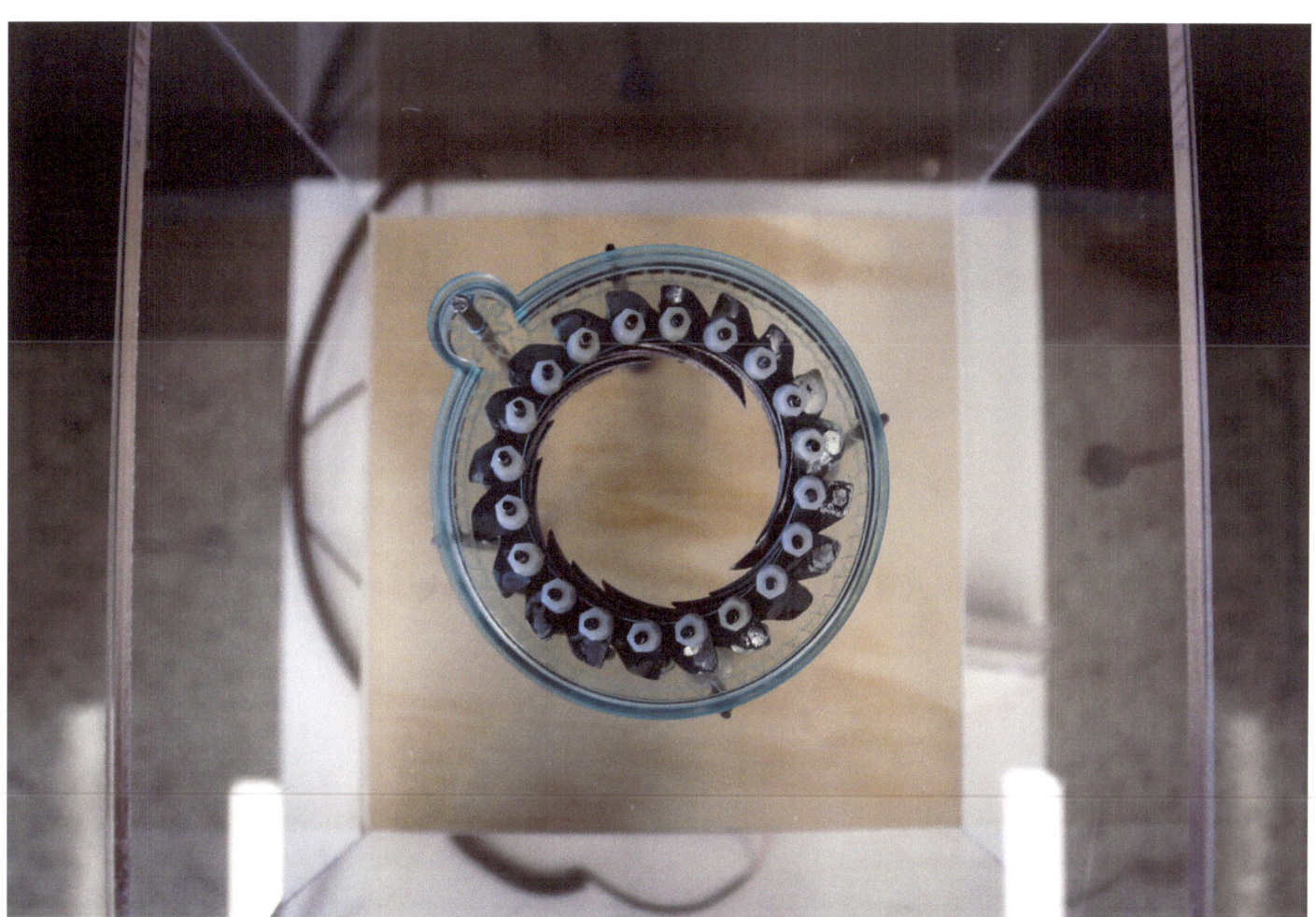

Trilogy

Pantea Karimi

Trilogy is composed of three rows of stands: Archive, Experiment, and Result. The installation is a response to Mary Shelly's novel Frankenstein; it tackles human desire to experiment with the notion of creation and to innovate new scientific methods to create new life. The stands display curious images of exploration into the properties of human body in medieval period (Archive), medical surgical tools as a metaphor for Victor Frankenstein's creation of a humanoid (Experiment) and the current and future research on stem cells and human embryos (Result)

Pantea Karimi works with installation, prints, virtual reality and video projection. Her work is an exploration into the pages of medieval and early modern scientific manuscripts, Persian, Arab and European and the long-term exchange of scientific knowledge across these cultures. She examines how illustrations in ancient scientific manuscripts played a role in communicating knowledge and how the broader aesthetic considerations of science were closely related to art. Karimi has exhibited her works in diverse solo, group and traveling exhibitions in Iran, Algeria, Germany, Croatia, Mexico, the UK, and the United States.

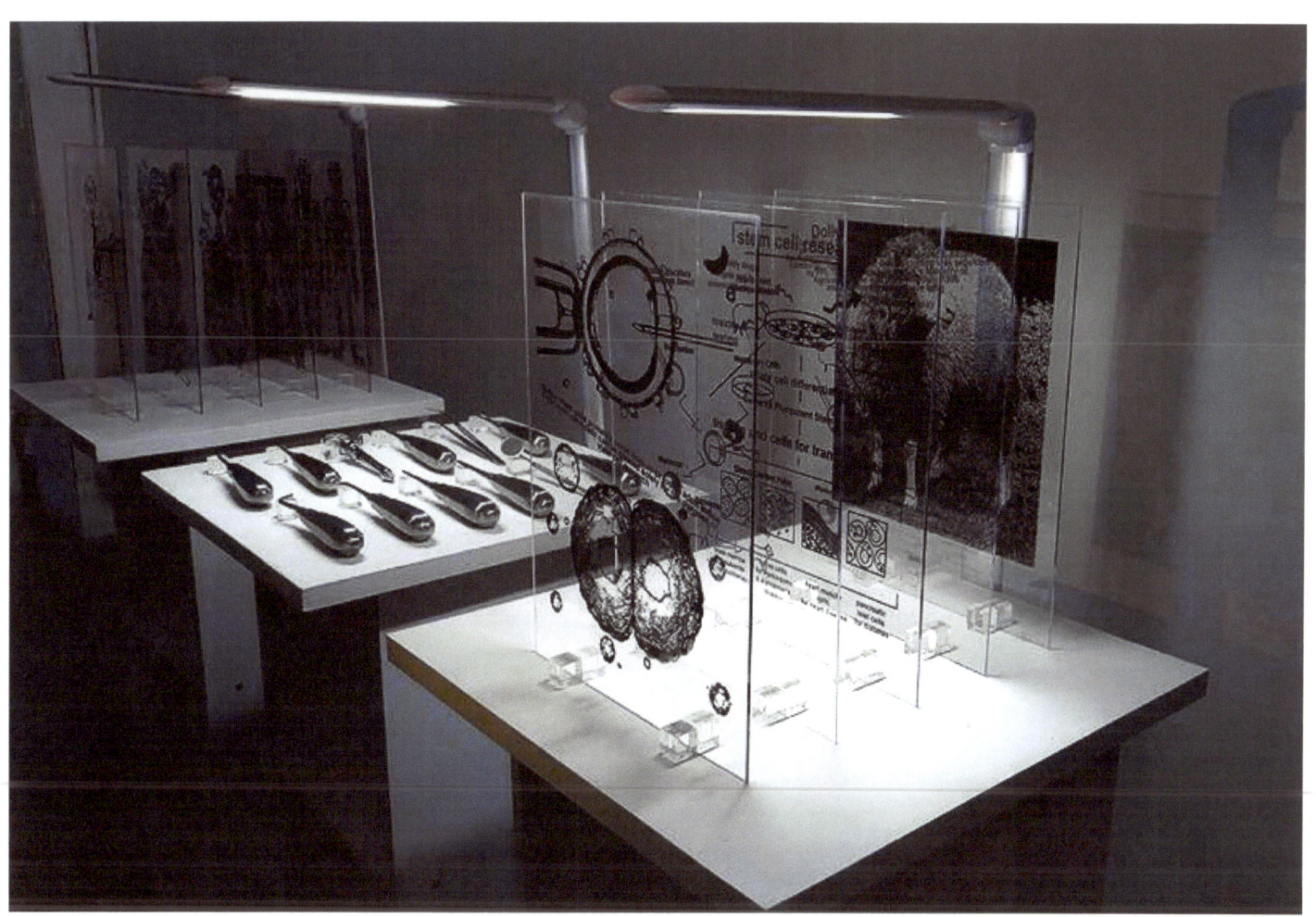

The More The Merrier

Jiaqi Zhang & Anton van Beek

The More The Merrier invites audience to place as many magnets as possible into the slots. Common human emotions; joy, surprise, excitement, and frustration will emerge, and be amplified while more magnets are added. By using statistical inference, the sound system identifies a series of rapid emotion changes real-time recorded from the previous players, building a sharable reservoir of emotion experience generated by intersecting vocal expressions. The piece intends to highlight the commonness that we all share as human beings through the similarity of our feelings, no matter the race, gender, or class; we are the same in this challenge.

Jiaqi Zhang is an interdisciplinary artist who explores the dynamic relationship between people, technology, and space. Her interests lie in the similarity and distinction of sensory perception and emotional experience in everyday life.

Anton van Beek is an engineering student whose academic interests focus the interface of mechanical engineering and artificial intelligence. With "childlike" excitement his work explores new developments in these fields.

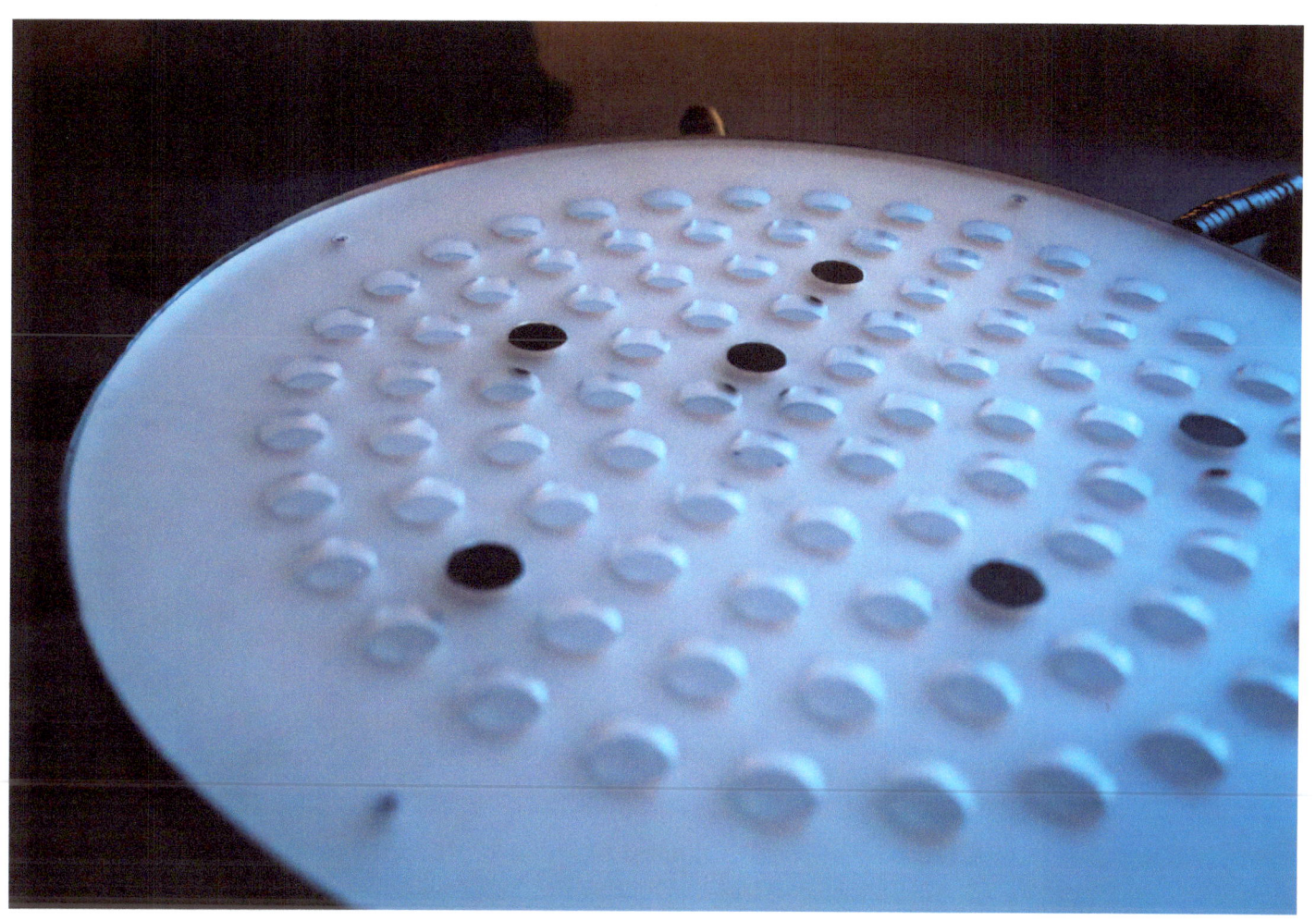

Deep Dream Vision Quest

Gary Booddhoo

Behind this screen is a neural network that hallucinates on the world it sees through a live camera, reconstructing input with visions from its own memory. Movement activates each new dream cycle, and the hallucination intensifies the longer its field of vision is motionless. Standing in front of it, you will see creatures emerge from suddenly alien landscapes, only to fade the second you move.

Interaction designer Gary Boodhoo turns neural networks inside out to make pictures of minds. A machine learning enthusiast, his creative practice encourages emotional connections with smart objects viewers can no longer distinguish from themselves.

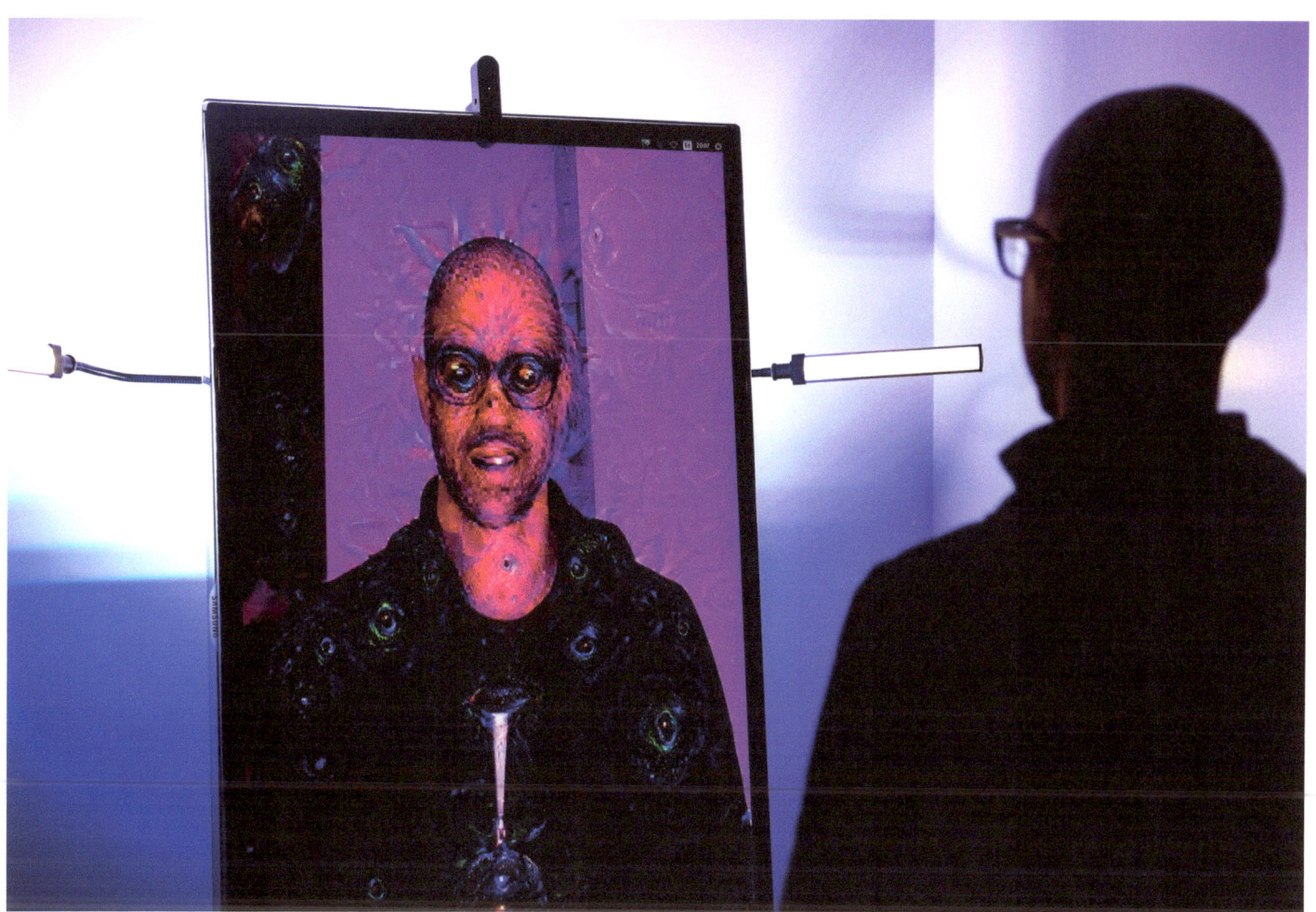

iAltar

Brian Reibolt

iAltar is a continuous, autonomous computer controlled video and sound art installation: a networked system of small computers that sends a query phrase of random words to the Google image search engine, displaying the phrase and the resulting images on video monitors while using an artificial voice to speak the phrase. It is accompanied by a musical background generated by a music algorithm using sound samples created by the artist.

Brian Reinbolt studied music (piano performance) in Florida and he obtained an MFA in electronic music at Mills College. At the turn of the Millennium, he started working on various multimedia projects involving electronic circuitry. In an effort to make the projects solidly presentable, he taught himself woodworking and is currently creating electronic timekeeping devices.

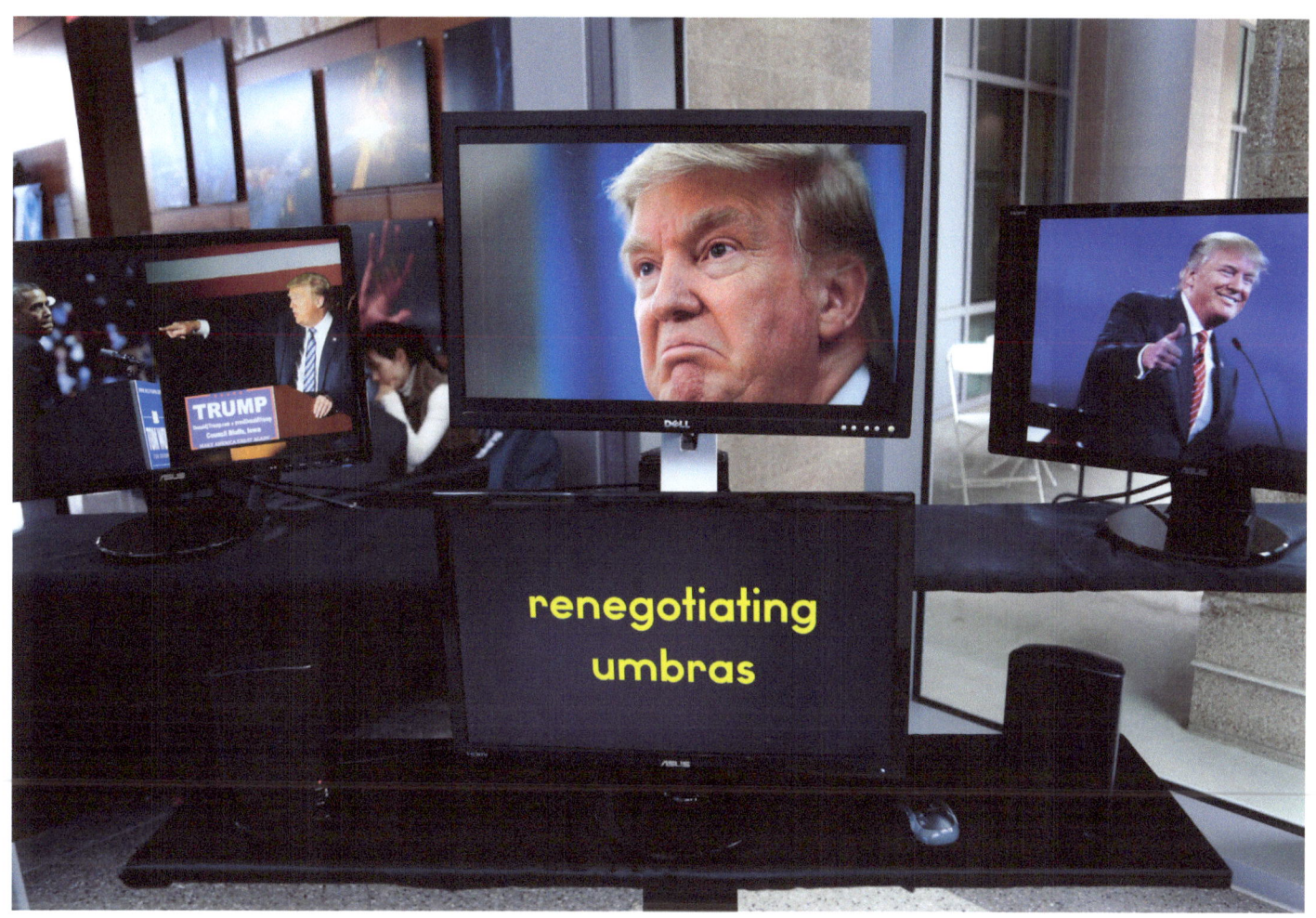

Lost In Google Translation

Purin Phanichpant

Neither humans nor machines are perfect. While the Google Translate algorithm can translate phrases across a wide range of languages instantaneously — something that extremely few humans are capable of, its accuracy might never be able to catch up with the subtleties of human languages that it tries to work with. These discrepancies become evident when a phrase is first translated (in this case, into Thai), and then re-translated back into English. These shortcomings in both humans and machine's capabilities point to the future where both parties coexist and collaborate.

Purin Phanichphant is a San Francisco, California based artist and designer. With his roots in northern Thailand, where he spent part of his life as a Buddhist monk, combined with his background in designing innovative products in Silicon Valley, Purin's interactive objects and installations engage audiences while exploring authenticity, expressiveness, and co-creation. His media often incorporates buttons, knobs, and screens, combined with a touch of code, resulting in simple, playful, and interactive experiences for the audience.

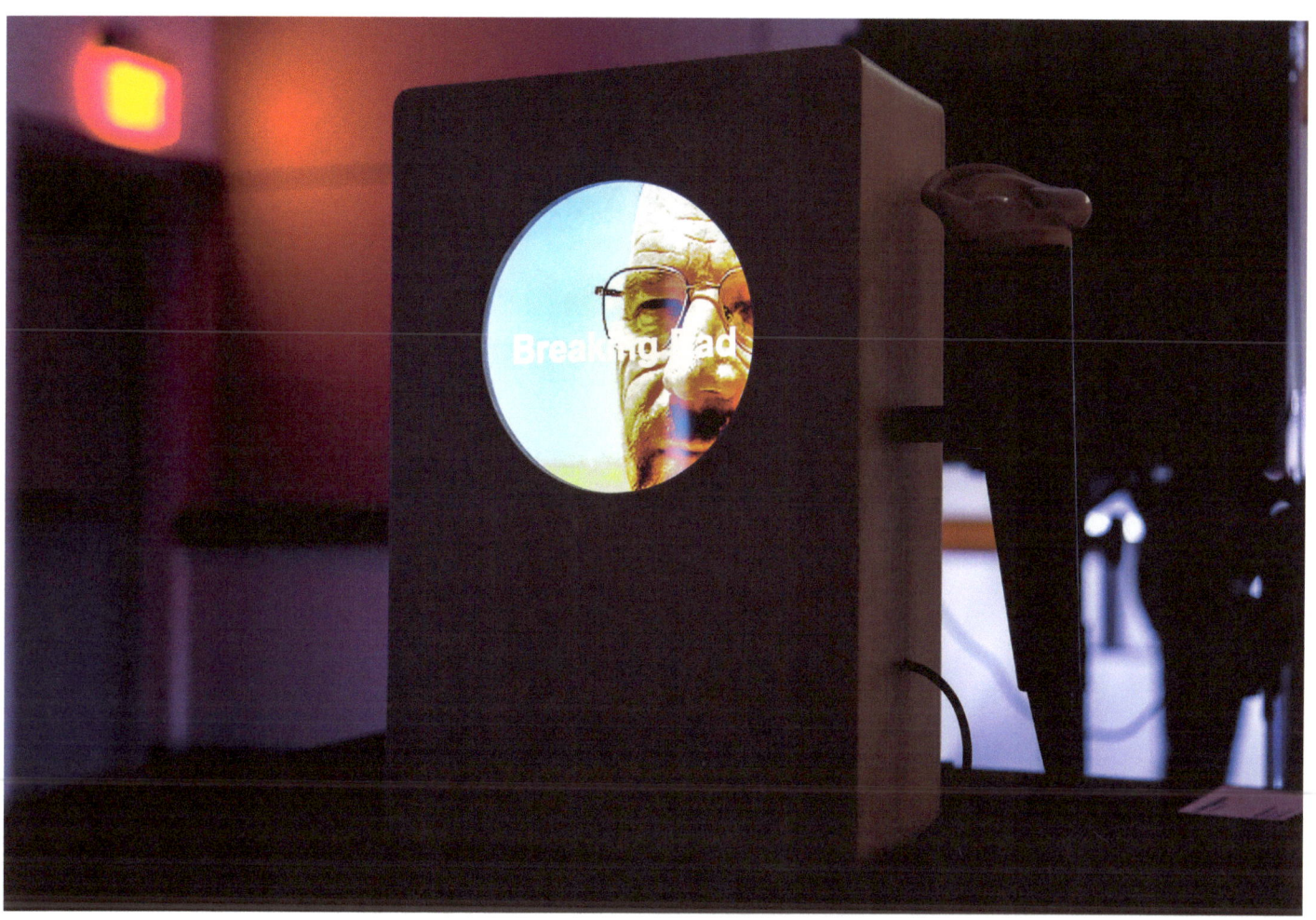

Liquefied Realities:
Evolving Between

Raul Altosaar

Experienced anew by every viewer, Liquefied Realities is an interdisciplinary experiment constructed to bypass traditional modes of artistic engagement. Woven by hand out of the disparate remnants of emerging technologies, this liquefied VR environment invites deep interaction and continuous co-creation.

Raul Altosaar resides in the shadows beneath disciplines, counterintuitively improvising with ambient technologies. He works alongside intelligent machines to protect and explore the emergence of novelty across domains. In other words, he endeavors to birth beautiful, impossible things.

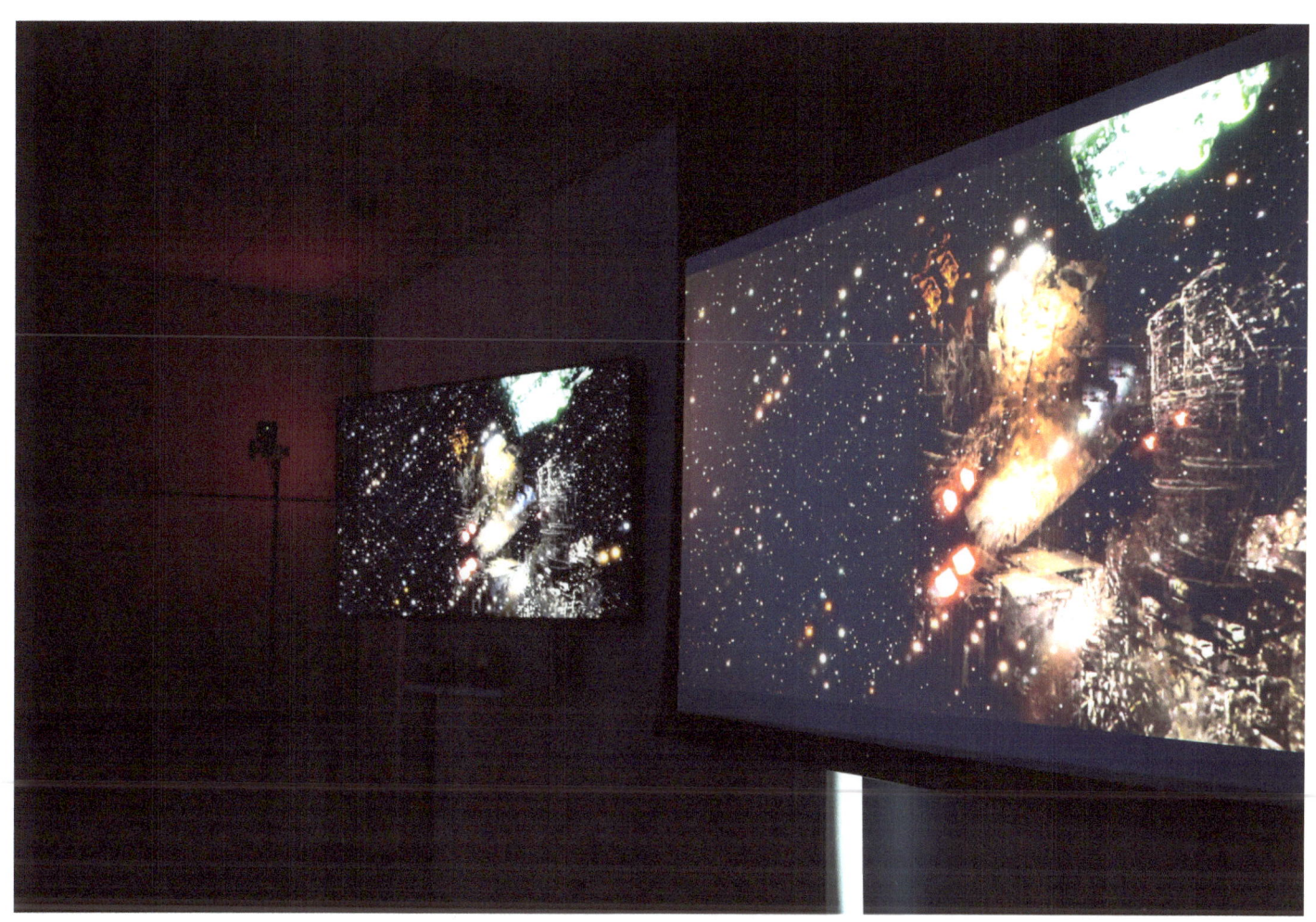

Static Electricity Sculptures

Anja Ulfeldt

The work in this series conjures a connection to preternatural phenomena such as St Elmo's Fire and Franklin's Bells. In keeping with the event's Frankenstein theme, the work is brought to life by electricity and implies just a touch of danger. These experiments explore the history and discovery of electricity through encounters with static charges.

Anja Ulfeldt is an interdisciplinary artist, teacher, and curator working primarily in sculpture and time based media. Time and presence are the consistent themes of her work, particularly the presence of the audience. Ulfeldt's work addresses psychological relationships to human infrastructure through visual art, sound, and durational experience.

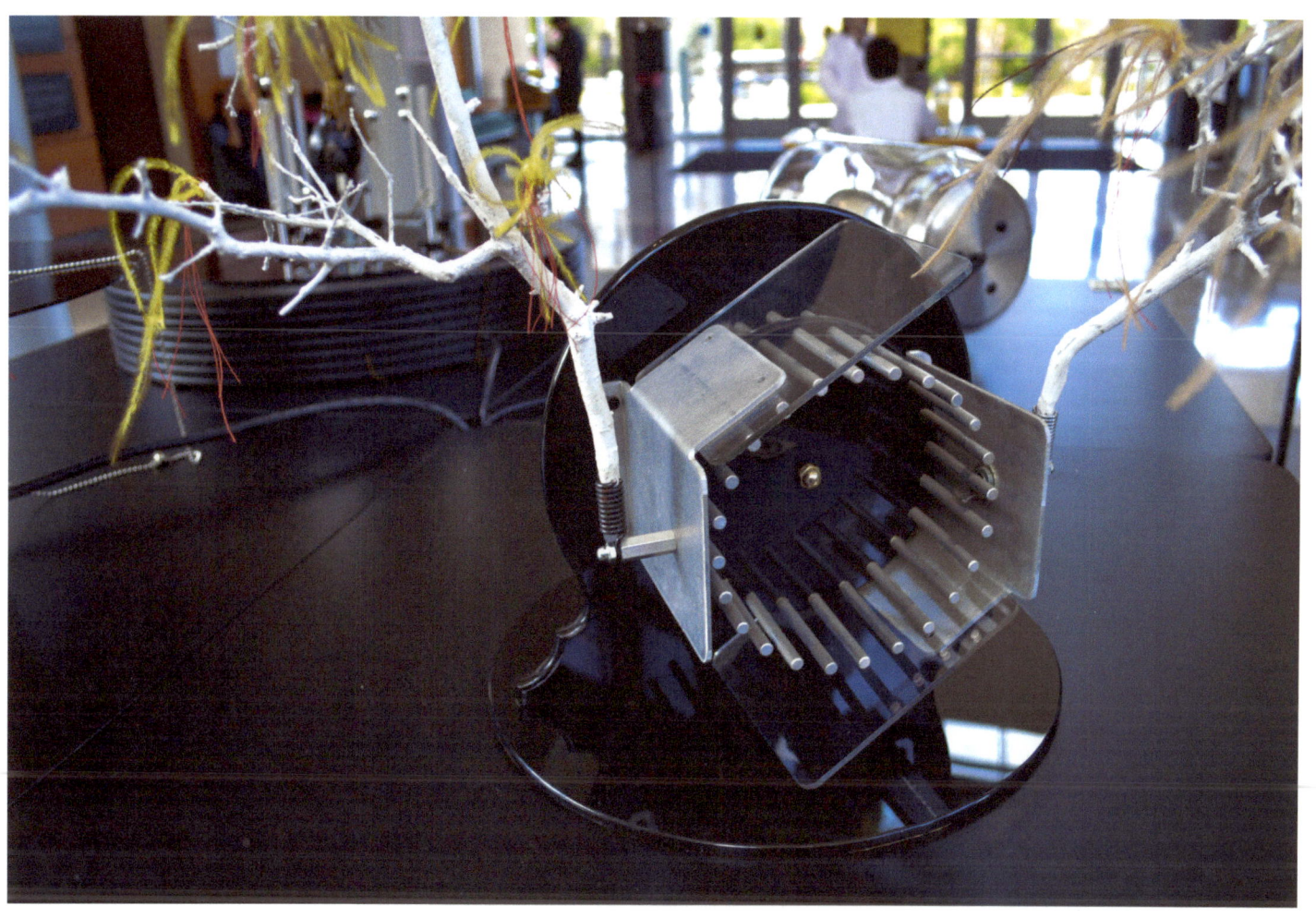

The [ECO]Nomic Revolution: When Microbiological Logic Determines Everything

Cesar & Lois

The [ECO]Nomic Revolution: when microbiological logic determines everything is a project that alludes to humanity in the Anthropo/Capitalocene as the iconic Dr. Frankenstein, while also referencing the fear that microscopic cultures tend to elicit across humanity. In this case, the societal output (Frankenstein's monster) is an economic system that ignores nature's input. This project allows a conduit for nature's "micromonsters" to determine a new [ECO]nomy.

Cesar & Lois ponder autonomous systems that integrate natural and technological networks. In their various bodies of work, Cesar Baio subverts the algorithms of autonomous systems, while Lois (Lucy HG Solomon) infuses art with nature's data. Together they create fungal systems that tweet and posit nature-based economies. Project contributors include Scott Morgans, biologist at California State University San Marcos, along with CSUSM undergraduate researchers and artists: Kiana Ajir, Kodie Gerritsen, Mei-Ling Mirow, Derick Northington, and Stephen Rawding.

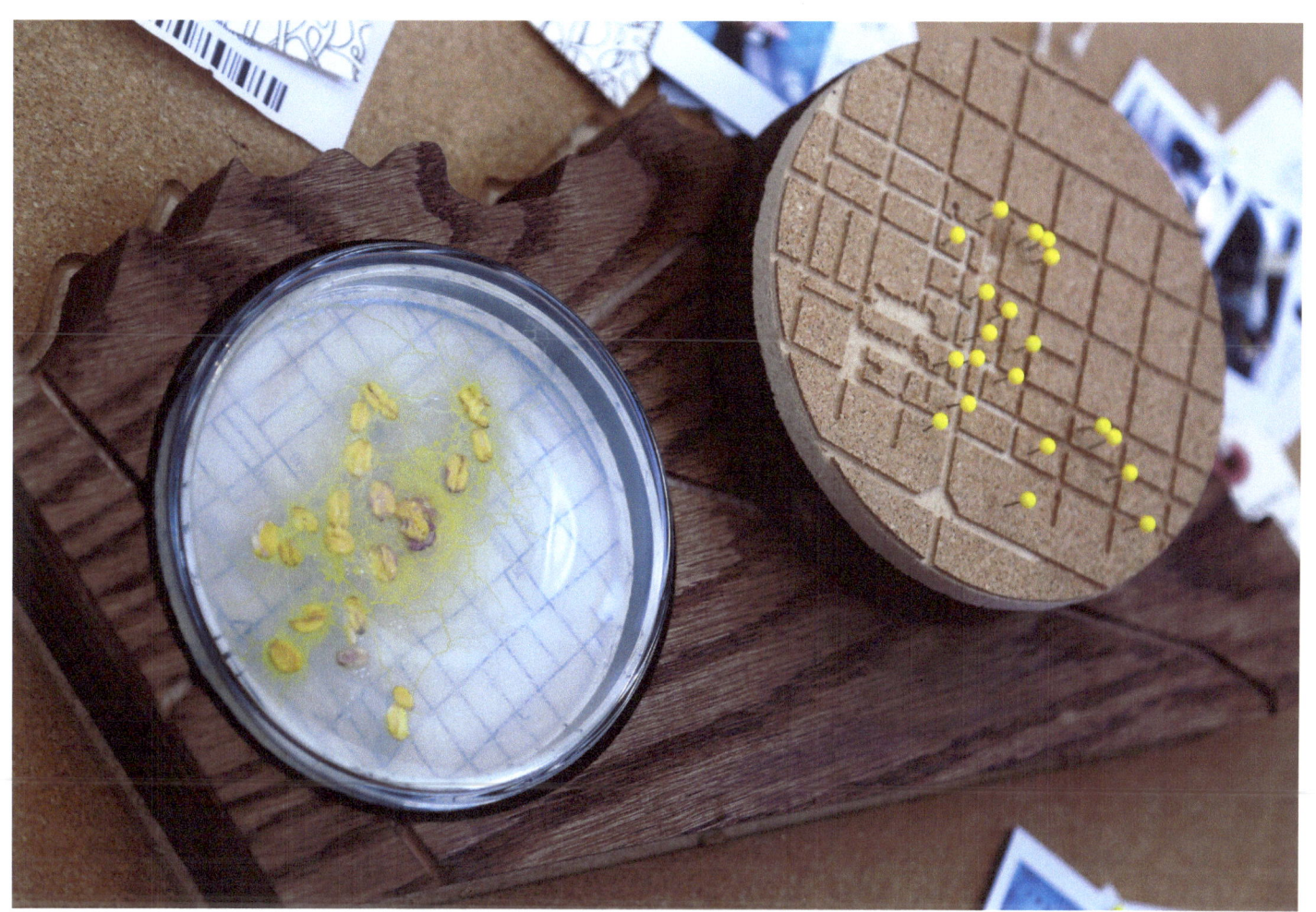

Re-thinking Extinction

Kathleen Deck

Re-thinking Extinction is a project that involves creating new solutions to current resolutions pertaining to climate change induced species extinction. Robo-tort, a robot prototype of the California Desert Tortoise (Gopherus Agassizii), created in collaboration with UCSC Professor Barry Sinervo, offers possibilities for ideas involving the repositioning of the California Desert Tortoise to engineer their migration with a robot shepherd to help inspire them to move north, thus providing a more natural migration process than forcefully

Kathleen Deck has sought innovative paths and connections between creativity and sustainability to develop her arts research practice at the intersection of art and science. She is a new media artist MFA candidate at the University of California Santa Cruz, interested in themes of sustainability, climate change and animal extinction.

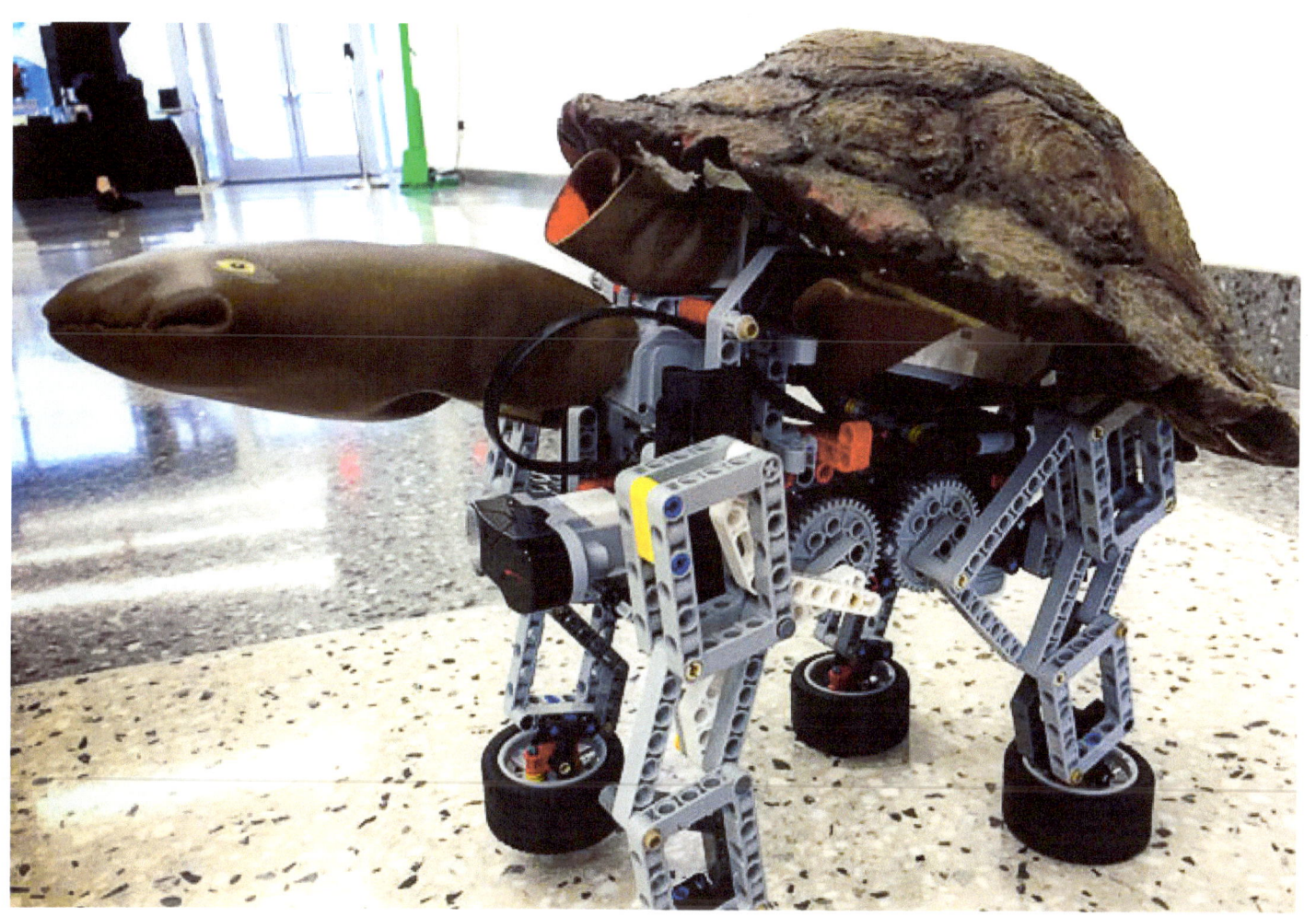

Off in the Distance, Act 1: Growing the Collection

Steve Durie

Off in the Distance is an artwork in which participants are invited to use familiar gestures of human- machine interaction. We have become accustomed to machines that watch our movements. Set in the desert one simply looks to create signs of life to try and make contact.

Steve Durie is an artist, and teacher who works mostly in electronic based sculptures and interactive systems. He is interested in variety of approaches for creating art work for public participation and collaboration to create joyful and insightful moments.

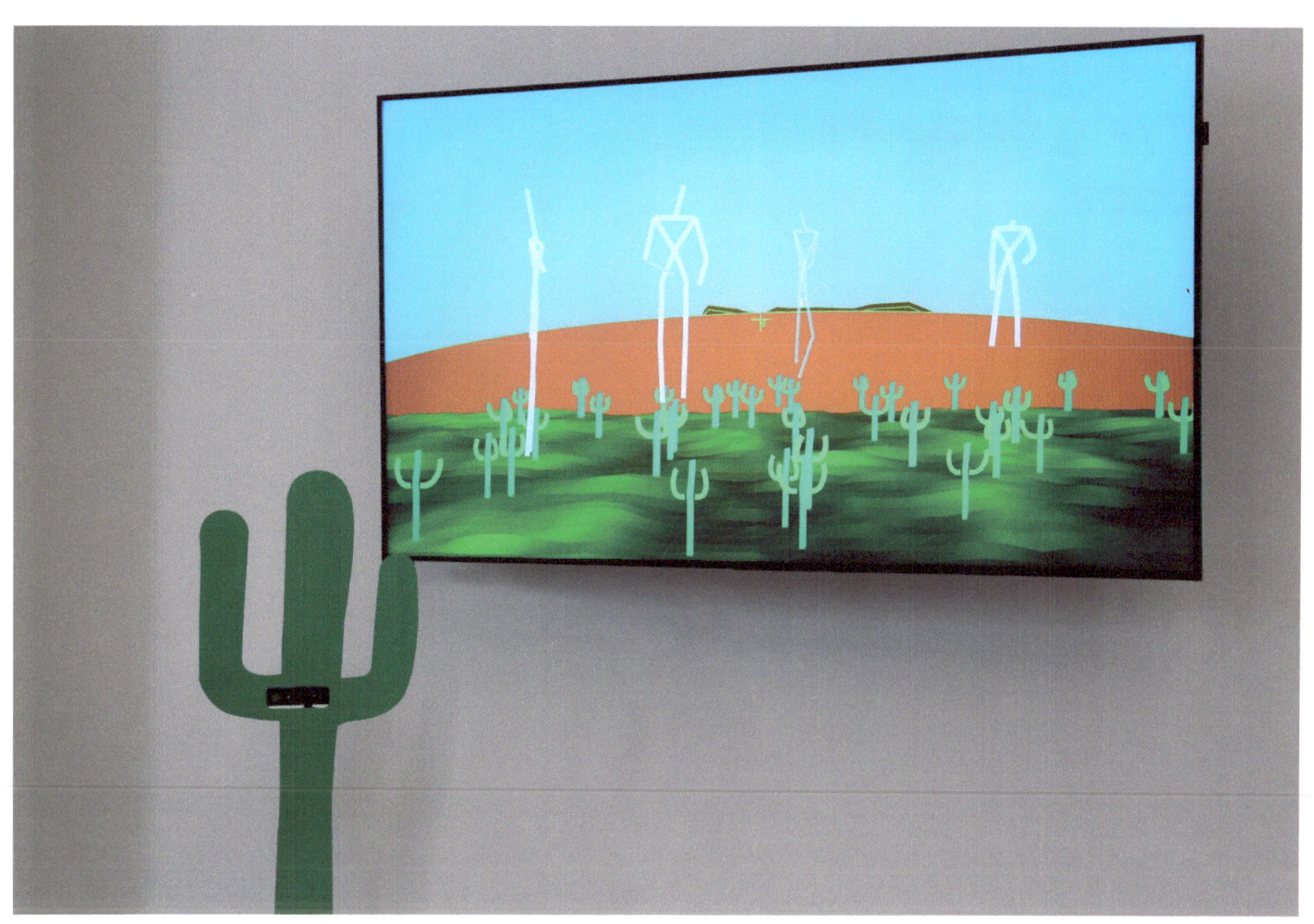

Microbial Sonorities Sonifying Bacterial Voltages

Carlos Castellanos

Exploring the use of emerging bioenergy technologies and ecological practices as artifacts of cultural exploration, Microbial Sonorities represents an inquiry into sound as a method of investigating the bioelectric and behavioral patterns of microorganisms.

Carlos Castellanos is an interdisciplinary artist and researcher with a wide array of interests such as cybernetics, ecology, embodiment, phenomenology, artificial intelligence and art-science collaboration. His artworks have been exhibited at local, national and international events such the International Symposium of Electronic Art (ISEA), SIGGRAPH & ZERO1.

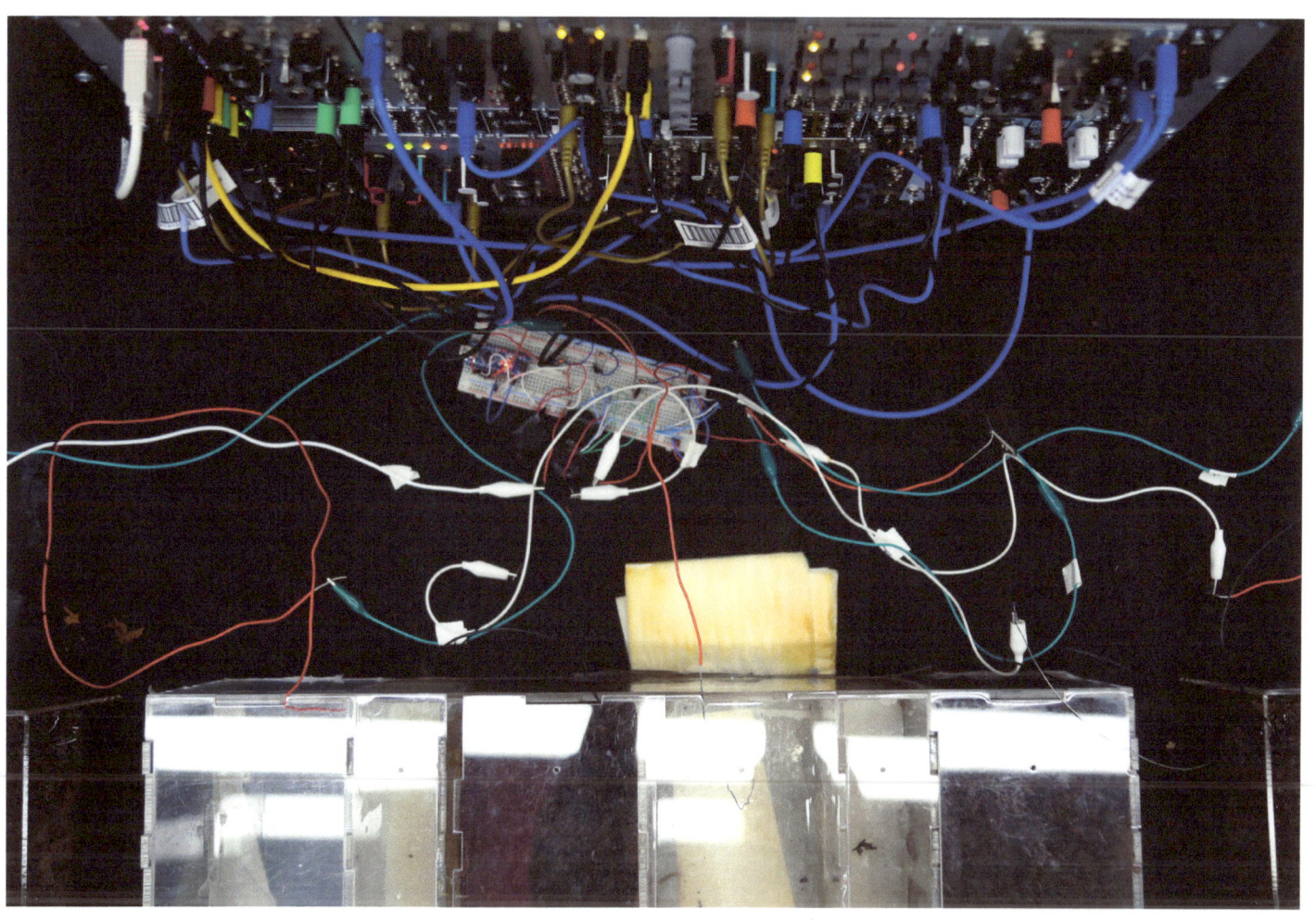

Feast of Eternity

Amy Karle

The time we are at in evolution is humanity and technology merging. Envisioned as an artifact of a speculative future, Feast of Eternity depicts a human skull, which typically represents death and mortality in conjunction with the possibility of growth and life embodied in one piece. Considering healing and enhancing, and questioning the role and possibilities of the body and technology merging was carried through the work. Exponential technologies, digital manufacturing tools, and workflows used in the medical field and biotech were leveraged in both concept and creation. The sculpture is created from reality capture, a 3D scan of a human skull, digital design and generative art. Pattern speculatively designed for direct skeletal implant, osseointegration and potential osteoconduction (dependent on materials used). Crystallization on the 3D printed form depicts how cells grow along the lattice and represent the mystery, delicacy and preciousness of life.

Amy Karle is an internationally award winning Bioartist whose work can be seen as artifacts of a speculative future where digital, physical, and biological systems merge. Karle's artwork taps what it means to be human and opens minds to future visions of how technology could be utilized to support and enhance humanity.

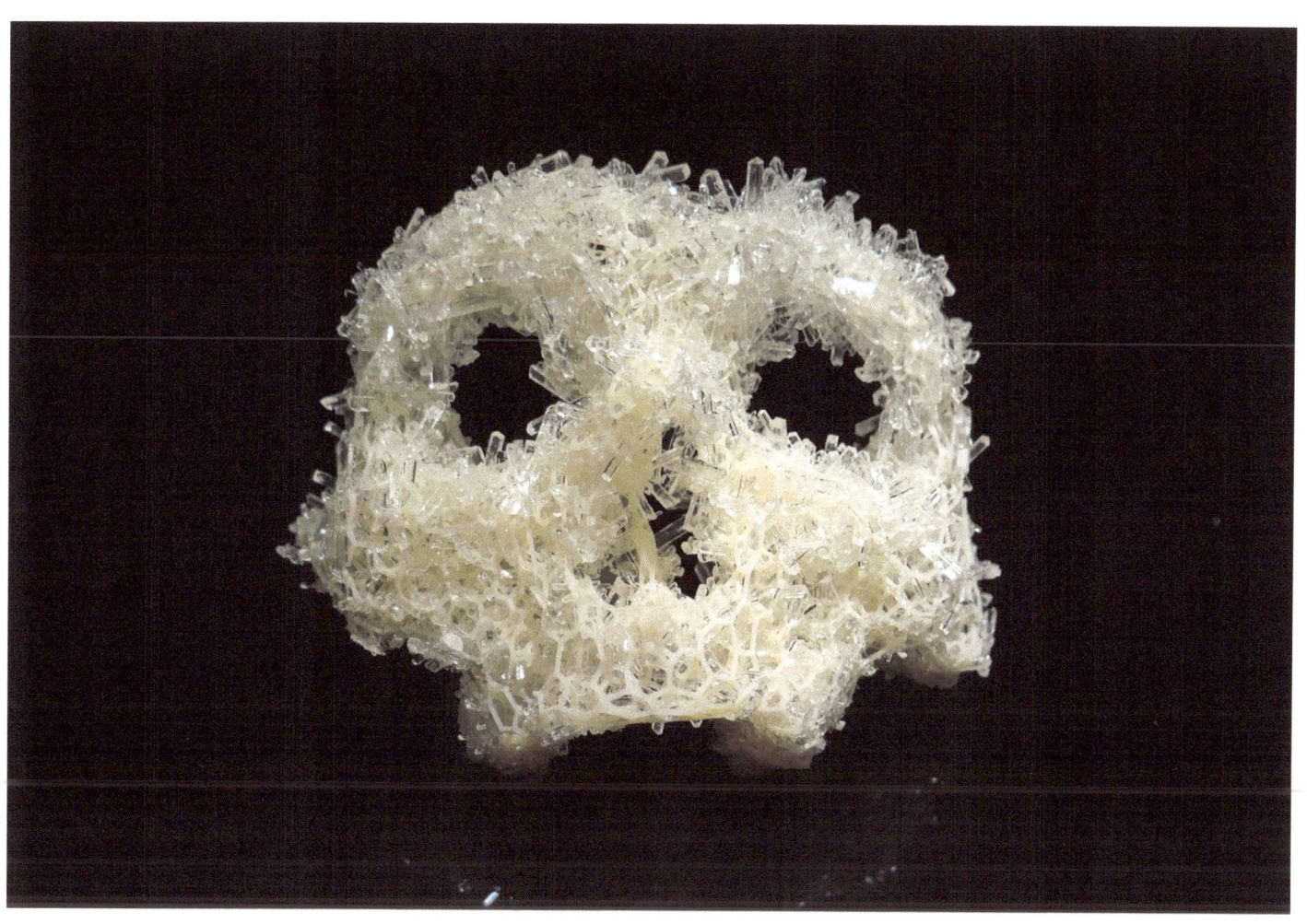

Carillon

Rob Hamilton & Chris Platz

Carillon (2015) by Rob Hamilton and Chris Platz is equal parts interactive musical performance environment and distributed virtual instrument. The core interactions in Carillon focus on the control of spinning gears - the heart of the carillon itself. By interacting with a set of gears floating in the rendered HUD – grabbing, swiping, etc. performers speed up, slow down, and rotate each set of rings in three dimensions. The speed and motion of the gears is used to drive musical sounds and instruments, turning the virtual /physical interactions made by the performers into musical gestures. Each performer controls their own sound, and in concert with other performers, that sound isspatialized around the hall.

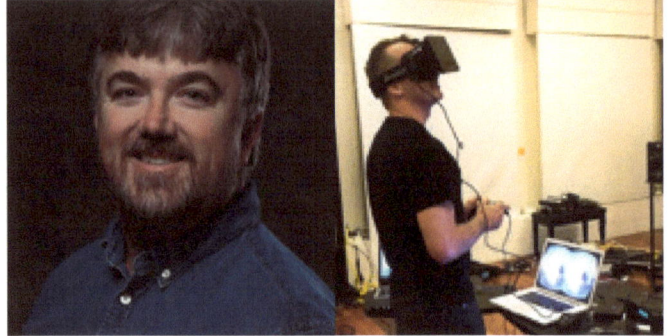

Rob Hamilton explores the converging spaces between sound, music, and interaction. His creative practice includes mixed-reality performance works built within fully rendered, networked game environments, procedural music engines and mobile musical ecosystems. His research focuses on the cognitive implications of sonified musical gesture and motion and the role of perceived space in the creation and enjoyment of sound and music. Dr. Hamilton received his PhD from Stanford University's Center for Computer Research in Music and Acoustics (CCRMA) and currently serves as an Assistant Professor of Music and Media at Rensselaer Polytechnic Institute.

Chris Platz is a virtual world builder, game designer, entrepreneur, and artist who creates interactive multimedia experiences with both traditional table top and computer based game systems. He has worked in the industry with innovators Smule and Zynga, and created his own games for the iOS, Facebook, and Origins Game Fair. His real claim to fame is making interactive stories & worlds for Dungeons and Dragons for over 30 years. From 2007-2010 Chris served as an Artist in Residence at Stanford University in Computer Graphics.

Andrew Blanton

Waveguide

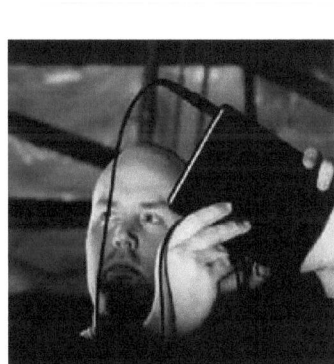

Waveguide is an audio visual performance that uses the internet as a resonant body for drums. By sending data from drums to a server and back through the audience's cell phones in real time, the work uses the array of cell phone speakers to create an immersive audio visual environment. Conceptually, the work draws on a number of different topics exploring the ubiquity of cell phones in contemporary society, and what it means to have an increasingly mediated reality through the screen of a smart phone. Each phone of the audience acts as an individual small speaker, screen, and interactive environment, allowing for real time dispersed audience interaction with the work as it is performed.

Andrew Blanton is a percussionist, media artist, and educator. He is currently the area coordinator of the Digital Media Art program and CADRE Media Labs at San Jose State University. His work is fundamentally transdisciplinary combining classical percussion, new media art, and creative coding to create realtime sonic and visual instruments. He has shown his work all over the world including Google Paris, the Studio for Electro Instrumental Music in Amsterdam, University of Brasilia, and the 20016 International Symposium for Electronic Arts in Hong Kong among many others.

Team

Wu Bin | coordination
Emily Bright | art curator
Maria Cerrone | communications
Sandra Corzantes | administration
Anna Davidson | master of ceremony
Roya Ebtehaj | media
Curtis Frank | advisory board
Leslie Jaramillo Koyama | advisory board
Rieko Yajima | advisory board
Sofia Lozano | Program Development
 & Educational Outreach
Jinxia Niu | event management
Saumyaa Saumyaa | advisory board
Piero Scaruffi | festival founder
Joel Slayton | art curator
Grace Macphail Taylor

SLAC

Rachel Isip | Outreach and Events Manager
Angela Anderson | Public Relations
Molly E. Zatarain | Event Event Specialist

Sponsors

SLAC National Accelerator Laboratory
Stanford Medicine and the Muse
China Thinkers Bureau
GES International Culture Exchange
ZERO1
American Arts Incubator
Stanford Office of the Vice President for the Arts
Stanford Office of Science Outreach
Dean of Engineering
Dean of Humanities & Sciences
Dean of Medicine
Dean of Earth, Energy & Environmental Sciences
Thymos Foundation

www.ingramcontent.com/pod-product-compliance
Lightning Source LLC
Chambersburg PA
CBHW042323250526
R18347300001B/R183473PG45473CBX00025B/25